Hey~Oka

foolish wolves know secrets

TERESA WRIGHT

Chaos, like a teacher, leads stray wolves,
to places of their own.
Undeterred by those strings and veils
that plant our feet in these parts,
this cluster,
bird dogs feed.
Blood that talks to children
after its time,
mothers who deliver children,
safely to the forest,
where unwavering allies
are reborn of
the compost.

DEDICATED

in unconstrained reverence, to the memory of:
a gossamer sister,
Catherine Ann Murphy (1962 – 1970)
an imperfect mother,
Marianne Isobel (Thibault) Murphy (1939 – 2005)
a better-late-than-never aunt,
Stephanie Carol (Thibault) Ramsay (1947 – 2011)
an equal vibration,
Kimberly A. (Ramsay) Vandenberg (1967 – 2017)

CONTENTS

Patted Backs   i

The Heyoka   ii

2   WE, THE PEOPLE   1

3   A COZY ROCK   20

4   MIRROR IN THE BATHROOM   30

5   LANDING   50

PATTED BACKS

To all the souls who've put up with this odd manifestation of life, I am grateful. I am more sponge than rock, and have soaked in every learning that has scratched my human surface, wafted into my nostrils, or forced its way down my throat.

I have already experienced fifty spins around the sun, obviously then, there are a multitude of folks who have shaped the person I am today. Every one of them is, in some way, responsible for this collection.

There is a smaller, select group who have travelled longer roads, or swam oceans, with me. That tribe, they are a sequence of eventualities, they have prepared me. They have flavoured me with ripe ingredients, stirred, kneaded and proofed, all that was nothing.

Most notably, I must give thanks to my daughters' Katlynn, Zoe & Mackenzie for smashing me face first into the mirror, I would have neither breath nor words without each one you.

Aussi, quelle qu'un qui demand beacoup, mais jamais trop, des bisous!

The Heyoka

The Lakota, and other tribes, believe in a sacred conduit to forces that defy comprehension. That conduit, a human whose behavior is so backwards, his actions so absurd, exemplifies the irony, the mysterious duality that is the universe. To the Lakota, this was Heyoka, a sacred clown, a foolish wolf, the ultimate mirror. He had a paradoxical, contrary nature that was as revered as it was feared.

The Heyoka were ridiculous, comical, and sometimes obscene, and dressed the part, wearing bizarre and ludicrous clothing, makeup and accessories. They were thought to be fear and pain less, trusted as healers and interpreters of dreams. They were like flashes of lightning, their sudden outbursts and disturbances were likened to enlightenment, in the manner of the irrational acts of Zen masters in Japan.

Through physics, we know the dual nature of electricity means, while an object can carry a positive or negative electric charge, the electron is concurrently a wave and a particle. Early civilizations intuitively understood nature's duality. The Heyoka embodied this dual spiritual nature through tragicomedy, or joy united with pain, inseparable, as is the dual nature of electricity.

Stories passed down, speak of the Heyoka having been touched by divine power, similar to the old wandering fools in Europe. In the chaotic and absurd world today, the Heyoka is a hard fool to spot. But, trust me, they are nearby.

1 WE, THE PEOPLE
long, long ago ... we opened Pandora's Box

Here are poems about us. Oh, we are people! The greatest species of creatures. Imagine yourself an outsider, can you? Oh, we people must look odd to the rest of the universe!

Collected in this section are conversations about mankind, the human race, the infestation: who we are and who we think we are. Contemplate what we've done, where we've been, and where we are headed ...

Some considerations for reading this section: Pronouns are but little floppy disks – placeholders for the protagonists and daemons of Your imagination. I is unlikely to be me, I could be You. I might have been an army or a nation. You could be He, The could be Me. You could be I. I could be the cold war or the industrial revolution, or the evolution of the domestic cat.

We
are flexed
and fluted campers.

Herding peripheries
I jab them
senseless
chip at rough edges
sketch
soft diamonds

We
were toothed
cardboard. We will
divvy
the current.

First, my eulogy

First, I am a snowflake
impassive as blue lace,
as hell, just begging to
be salted to the gallows.

Next, I am an inglenook
responsive as hot sex
as heaven, pleading for
hail to ward off coffins.

Finally, I'll be a red light
guiding as fresh napalm,
as trigger fingers, luring
applause for my eulogy.

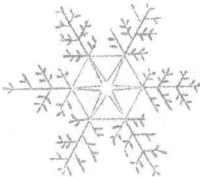

Should Orion Sleep?

Further down lines: dirty water –
still hot, dumps down
and out, so-called drinkable
airs.

The busy path seized the hungry loon, feet crunched tense underbrush
to bits, a hawk's wheezing bones knit a scarf.

Off roll rubber heads. Uppity
index fingers, hands,
benignly throw taut
bouquets.

Plastic doorbells rang up and down the goose, pulled her feathers with
drive-thru indulgence, kindly skinned bears gnarled Orion's belt.

Finer senses, seated behind
bloodshot spectacles
following gourds, offer
lunches.

Harder stars whispered to countless moons, slapped eternity silly with
arms and legs, dressed pulsars in heartfelt beaver pelts.

Desperate lakes, if we could
drown our never-saids,
lean-to links, we'd die with
words.

Numb snowflakes purred, fought the night with a deliberate veil.
Hearing trails, the owls smirked, wolves met our bones on the other side.

Fertile waters begin tender
feeding. All good
constellations set with
suns.

Right Angles

I swear it was there, over at the right curb.
I swerved, hard as I could, to the left.

Maybe it was road kill, not yet dead, but
waiting. Waiting to be gaped at an obtuse
angle. In early morning, I overheard the
engines muting to a standstill, fading
like your addiction, heading off to school.

Provoked, my head motored into reverse,
backed out of that alley, to where it all began.
Did I call you that night, from the scene?

I swerved, I know. But shouldn't
you wonder where I went wrong?
Knowing all about wrong and right,
feels slight, too much polish for me.

Your laugh is one grotesque tv. I hold you
back, so the surface like a polar dog falls
behind the brim of your nightcap. A flash,
it creeps tension into the yellow dawn
while a somber sheet cradles my easy pity.

A hoot spins my face. Looking awful in
light, an off-color slant, I caw spittle off
starving lips, lips dry as un-syruped pancakes.
I bide time like a knapsack studying war.

In front of me, normal twists a joke.
Living screws; stripping threads. Swerving
served up breakfast to the homeless, and
I feel a funny bone left inside; I burst a gut.
I ingest an comic's oblique crotch.

Soon upon a drunk stem

A milk-winged, bingo-faced dove
circles upward, striving,
striving upward bares puce feathers,
ever weighted, obliges sniffy-farts.

A moss-eyed, jet-petting lynx
sidles backward, creeping,
creeping backward wears duster-knucks,
ever twisted, obliges tin-tigers.

A garnet-palmed, polar-nubbed dude
schemes sideward, lapsing,
lapsing sideward spares gaping hearts,
ever fitted, obliges twitter-cats.

A teal-eyed, piggish-tailed chick
hops forward, skipping,
skipping forward glares on mass screens,
ever suited, obliges wafer-dolls.

A chrome-lipped, gas-guzzling bug
drowns downward, shifting,
shifting downward dares skid marked tombs,
ever cited, obliges two-cent-drones.

Thanksgiving Mathematics

Fiddly games, those antiquated ones with palpable trimmings, that kettle you into the arms of the maniac who grins and tallies integers naked.

Bared figures, unburdened since Len granted twice the glory. Vladimir thought to rally In ideas, then John sang On, bent against your good work.

A deuce coupled, a yoke doubled, a pair twinned, a bi-fold twosome, a duplicate duet – heaped or swept, no matter. Still a fitter seared or branded, makes four highly composite.

An objection on all fours, four-eyes on the four-door, a four-flusher: a foul four-letter-man minus one becomes a pickpocket driven by four horsemen, do the math! Increase give by thank, or upsize it.

So contemporary is sentiment. So up-to-date is tradition that publicly thanks the ranks swallowing American pies and sentimental stuffings, streamed with gravy.

Further north we swallow fairy tales like air, with a crush on our big brother. They kill two birds, we kill two birds, so on and on and so on, drinking diversity on the rocks.

Thanksgiving is an equation, a reckoning, a price tag. An invocation greater than a turkey and less than harvest pumpkin pie. If it wore grace around its neck and gratitude across its chest it would ride the bus to absolution eight turns past your every-day clock.

If it abandoned tradition, took leave of feast, shook off the groupies tailgating in driveways with deep-frying-smokers you would taste it vanilla as ice cream.

Swollen-soft synonyms watered down its full-bodied, unvarnished flavour like morning mugs, with toast and blameless obligation. Feasting ate need but glutted want, as pleased pumpkins graced the orange flames that easy-baked turkeys. Two birds stuffed, stoned cold with duty.

Yielding an abundance torn from stale bread multiplied the occasion. Wearing a feathered past: oldsters begged gods for pumpkins, dragged bones out for a soup full of wish; tables spread.

Giving fossils divided fruit equal to the many. Now gods, at odds, shout family-friendly expletives across the 4G, lowering costs and expediting free delivery. Elastic credit taps never-minding empty pockets.

cracks

Two plus two is fifty – fifty, to
some measures.

Divvying dutch,
collects consent on a rusted bus.

Cimmerian hours brag, eyeball
silver spoons.

A caliper, to gag spotless implants,
tiptoes up to frank. Weigh-scales
scrub his square peg with eggnog.
Spots splish-splash an unborn
master card, unfolding like a
middle finger. The fandom wallow
in smarting, crushing velvet laps.

Binary shadows hunch close to
well-dressed pet rocks, tethered
to a keen drunk at a tellus kiosk.

Whispers on lashes

Be glad you aren't the best in the universe. Not the nicest, strongest, anti-quacking speckle of dust-in-the-wind star, or That guy – in the world, the space of all that matters.

In a spliffy, thru the smoke I heard my voice strong as whispering: "Hey there, boy. Never stop dreaming, don't touch-down like Earth, but come back to me a lovely, lovely creature. (No un-dreaming) I'm youTube. Speechless.

What-what-what? I am watching you asleep, on the blacktop beside nefarious greens pushing out from under the cracked topcoat. You, a living tale, speaking of your greatness, of your what upon. Your what upon tweets in the spaces of all matters.

(If I didn't smoke I'd see you like an empty icon: devoid, well-mannered-stock stuffed inside the pockets of your hot-pressed watch.) Ever mind your artful factions, as Jesus at the shoreline.

Buying your shirts on eBay to trim their hands-free phones nifty, they eat your avatar like fish on tuesday. Call it Jesus, or trump it like playing cards shouting Go Fish. Prodigal mankind loafing.

Am I contained in space or constrained by Earth? Here nor there. Oh, potential speaks greek to natives, cree to french, arabic to americans. laughing-out-loud, in little l's. Outside, packed boxes grow ideas, invent new limits and forget where we came from.

Am I a real god if you can't touch me or text me over drinks? I wear looking eyes that calm the collective, a voice that sings like a worldwide messiah. There nor here, I post equality, a stepladder eclipsing stars as they rain on oceans. Twittering, I regurgitate you. It amuses me into salvation.

Faith, 140 types, lets your breathing eyes partake, your groupies drone, to grip its strange spongy heart. Trans-fat baby legs crawl an unabashed share of swallowed dreams. A generation glides by on laidback ignominy, cruises past gray pines dabbed along the gasping river, raising lofty crosses born absolute, wrapped cozy in uncertain heirloom quilts.

We, The Wanderers

Full moons tap out pure time, blow kisses
onto the earth, prod us to perish thoughts
that tack us to man-made boards where we
wait for our lines to be drawn. Drifting above
us, the cosmos knows us. Neighbouring stars
cluster like older gardens, from the days we
weeded by hand the sedatives, and steeped
night flowers, and drank all the docks, and
danced with barer feet. A home, above the
veil of carbon, drumming like a heartbeat,
unearthing the bones of our older selves.

Spirit Snakes

Beryl petals blush skivered on senile sky fade
dispatched elsewhere tick oppresses tock
watchers tab-keeping-down-pouring sheep
mutter hep flames lambasting crooning
sissing sere as fast as fiddling adders
much as soggy caskets hold on to
commotioned woolgatherings
the nighty-night   glow
stifles hush-hush

Hedged in   blank
drapes cradle pencils
sketching hairy shadows
across moons Stars tumble
next to the old vanilla threshold
that itchy nexus where dues are paid
to neighbours upright members collecting
zip-lipped under tables stained rose by frenzy
picked-clean bones train loads   stale nuts   typos
like us so far skirting best sellers Honed set jellyfish
jest barbed wire sheep jail muttonheads once moaning
idles   Blow   through fleece mitts ticks sip gross margins

in jack's hands

in his left hand, an older brush coats a moody deck.
in the air, winds whisk sweat, walloping other dads
raising flat brews to heaven, cheering the do-good-
enough ladies, who brutally smack wimps in mold.
heaps of needles wait by grown-up cedars. summer
skin. an ever-blue glass mirror wearing hairy coal.
its arms hold jack softly where his belt is polished.

his right hand wrings the pulp from a birch, like a
visiting whale, and dresses dead soldiers with wax.

in his left hand, one opaque girl ghosts. her breath
slips on comfort, she overheats a pound, burns and
mashes a greener bird. a tiara tickles knotted buns
offered up as leftovers. a middle button hurries. no
want beds the hidden pop-tarts or jack's soft wrist.

his right hand pets the wings of music, like a grey
gliding owl, and recalls dead soldiers with songs.

in his left hand, fistfuls of spaghetti swell. whiffy
cream flavours dry mushrooms. then white tender-
ness like a choice, reaches into a mouthful of un-
kissed crab. fingering the flambé of cheap cheese,
an ugly gold ring flogs. jack's soft knuckles bend.

his right hand pits the abscess in the crust, like the
mourning sun, and sweeps dead soldiers with wine.

in his left hand, private gold calves fix to lug iron
or clap rounds. suds washed down with clowns or
silver-spoon sports. pewter abc's stiffen limp bones.
cannonballs throb, considering our marrow a whirr,
a humdrum. a burial softly strokes jack's tired brush.

his right hand palms the left in his lap, like a coat of
silver sugar, and drinks dead soldiers in paper bags.

Yesterday's calamities had no hashtags

9/11/16 – It's a hashtag I Can't Believe It's Been 15 Years morning here; it blankets other parts of humanity in the evening or afternoon. Remembers and lest-we-forgets, most with pictures for impact, moving. Moving pictures. Moving words and gifs and sound bites. The cacophony of silence taken away upon the wings of AA #11, arranged. Still. Thunder. Blind. Sings. Rings. Sentences strung collected by internet, ash and paranoia. Loud. Aloud. Allowed, though truly a skyward claw by senior writers with rank and followers and retweets. Same as it ever was. Wipe out. Pay back. Blot out. Root out. All years push-pulling. King Charles on and off the bloody ottoman. Napoleon seesawing Allies. CCP to-and-froing the KMT. "Little Boy" mushrooming. Land of opportunity con land of liberty. Same. Uniform. Twin. Generic. Allied. Steady. Zero. Unfailing. Somber. It's a

damned shame. How many dogs were lost? Any count on birds, cats, iguanas? No body wants to remember that no soul remembers, far-off. Tall winds don't drag smoke onward. Not on and on. Weep. Off and on. Twitter. Hashtag tragedy. Cry. Till red-white-and-blue in the face. Face shallow graves buried twice beneath 1362 feet of urgent world trading and playschool and free enterprise. I hope they had their loved ones on their phones in pictures. Devices. Connections. American express. Come rain or shine or billowing ash – don't won't can't leave home without them. Breakthrough survival instincts: fight with flight. OR gone with evolution according to next-gen wisdom teeth. Evolved. Progress – mature. Build – throw together. Change – vacillate. Derive – judge. Cultivate – age. Elicit – extort. Materialize – objectify. Evolve – mushroom. Grow. All the in-betweens erased. Mankind. Kind. Kindness wipes out need. Needy soft middles. All the in-betweens. All the between the roof and the ground floors.

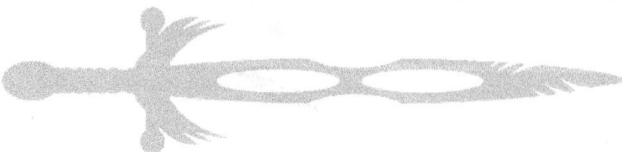

I am an itch called grace

I am a speck, an ectype: a head with tail; faint,

I yawn under sidewalks painted lickerish.

I am a fleck, an effigy: a finger excised; frigid,

I sense done doorsteps decorated allergic.

I am a bit, an instant: a hot-pressed hog; fancy,

I crush upon intersections schooled inattentive.

I am a whit, an infinity: a mocked mirror; flush,

I sing onto pigeonholes underscored mortal.

I am a tear, an ease: a bared fardel; familiar,

I crack inside smartphones blueprinted narrow.

I am a fear, an earth: a belly-up prayer; forsaken,

I swim near arteries ingrained unquenchable.

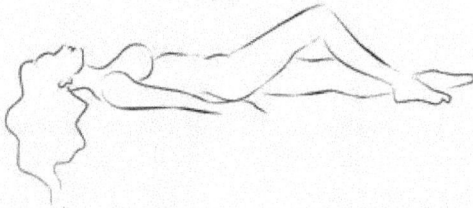

The Overdrawn Race

Two-timing! That time that gives out fudge, that leaks careful brown cocoa. Its easy spatters seduce blond-haired up and up text, one by one, so sallied bites blow out of line like fairy farts. Free, but needy airs steal fresh highchairs while lazy-boys tally crude see-through teeth and pirates trick maps of cloned fossils. Cut off, fake flies unpack keener games, fold pet thingamajigs. Opiate clocks sentry the figures cast upon the hill.

Vagabonds bearing unseasoned poetry schlep up and up. And up the hill they box at bossy go-cart-knuckling rabbits who puff up thin prickly chins. Whenever-shadows hold on, loiter in precise holes. One-two wed heroes wear bankrupt left cheeks. Right bruises throb under paper bones like virgins, bogged down under water, puzzling the unsung.

Fickle varnish: blah-blah prose rucks sublime jawbreakers, fires ugly pippin scrap, sews pods laced white and crusty, mops left-to-right, to stamp and skirt mildewed sandbanks, currents anchor goose meats and mince sardines for jelly; old coughs circle round and fresh strings wheeze.

Creaky rhymes giggle their dashed and gingered fingers, mixing up balmy and dilute lotion. Day-tripping kids crouch on the shore, nursing charms, set in candy rings by sobs of bedridden cursive pens. Oppidan lore showers their bellies. Wiz-pistols bob. They are barges that wave, shout ahoy! Crack bosses, who disinfect stone-ship carousels, guzzle, and wink.

A twice-cursed tot-mombie, baptized green, mends buttons with little pink shoestrings. She fixes, as new, her wormy carrot shrine. In a dream, she nags wall-to-wall quarters for a chronic nightmare. While lazing beside bus fare coins break and she inhales, or sucks up in-rage-boxes; kicking places, these days, smuggle ambitions and gravy cows thru quick check outs.

The fountain laughs at a bench crystalizing milk, her antagonistic stroller flicks be-happy's. Lately, frisbees fix her damp rubber feet useful: she slides farther away from virginity and lays alongside a sober marbled bed.

Her lying debit card lowers its voice: a strict sly drift tucked inside her boutique cleavage, doled out as soft candied ginger to shaven bare ass-dimpled shotguns. It buzzes and tickles her breast. Uncurious and out cold she lulls pocket-children with forkfuls: tasty forgiving bubble-gum-smelling-not-tasting left-over jelly donuts.

Sour-baby songs swallow the gangrene ginger-bread, too camp-fired s'mores hook-up to weld thoraxes, cauterize windpipes. Needled trails echo tagged tattoos. Sucked up, pulling bottles: rabbits piled two-deep on tied topping-boats.

Pack avoidance for easy travel

Fly.
Travel far for cheap fixings, gather airmiles.

Walk.
Veil paved boots petite with scattered bones.

Cruise.
Float like rhythm concocting a bobbing hook.

Run.
Bypass quick certainty, mist overseeing taupe.

Tour.
Cross iron rails so safekeeping feigns a hoot.

Rush.
Pace piers with tic-tacs begging fresher breath.

Step.
Phase, shift the burnt horizon as a learning curve.

Escape.
You deserve it; the coming wrinkle is too much.

I am an orb
as medicinal as chaos,
as glossy as a reflection.

I AM THE ONION

2 A COZY ROCK
The Cosmos drums this planet's news

Our Land, this spherical lump of magma and metals, rubble and reef, slate slabs and shelfs, spins on and on, upon its invisible axis, while tracing our calendar marking. We mark time with our human things. Who cares about the chicken or the egg – that's a diversion for our intellect, a question designed to prevent us from contemplating the complication that we, in truth, are.

Without humans ... would the skies be so noisy as to halt migrating birds? Would mechanical monsters eat goose meat? ... glassy sky-scrapers trick wings toward quick deaths? Would jungle cats and desert dogs spew their chemical addictions into waters, defiling and corrupting its native dwellers and bottom feeders? Would the forests revolt in masses, gulp Kool-Aid in groups, whining they're done with working for minimum wage? And so on... And on...

If it were not for this giving marble would we exist? This book, for one, would not! What dollars will matter if there is no food to buy? Trains, planes and automobiles will sink into hospitals, begging anti-depressants, without land to be travelled, explored, exploited. They will mourn us, buried beneath their rusting gears.

The poetry of this section worries about this earth that sustains us, that gave us life. Here are angry outbursts. Have a tete-a-tete with the oldest tree you know, touch it's rough and real bark, feel its constrained cool-headed energy. The physical world, real nature, as we know it, is dying for us to die.

Some considerations for reading: Remember the pronouns! Toronto could be Paris, a lake could be a puddle. I could be a race, or an old gorilla.

20

The could be Me. You could be I. We could be the third star on Orion's belt, or the west wind, or simply a domesticated feline.

Falling Heir to the Shore
considering the TRCA's Waterfront Project ...

The morning sun breaks a laugh over mounds of compost: creeping, less with thyme. Now testy, paid and sold by dog weed and garlic mustard.

Suppose our workadays patronized green canopies, weeded out nosy say-so goons, estimated vigor and fermented crimeless drinks.

Male Martins bank forward, play jeopardy with our gentile good-taste, double-crossing their Swallow mates, feathered sure and shameless.

Do we name them jailbirds on affairs? Spell them sleazy, unflappable, and bless their booting out, these done-for beach-bank-sentries?

All the while organized duds spat seeds like chunks of twice divorced concrete, whirled with blithe precision, swearing to waive the weather.

Imagine we conditioned our wear and tear. Never married. Nevermore done-deals. Buried excrement beneath our bones.

On the verge of Lake Ontario gangs of rebar sunbathe like wild rebels forgoing SPFs and PPEs, snubbing libel and vexing social medicine.

This afternoon, I dreamt on the lake, under the intact moon: sunburnt and rusted long-arms forfeited muddy real estate for pure preference.

Nearer to Orion's feet than yesterday are brighter stars. They know what's coming: for to name a constellation, the gauge and cadence ticks off.

Pull up a chair Orion, sigh our calling once, past regret. Ignore today when clocks trumpet in nests of AWOL-bees, and call upon mute wings.

So, spill full stars like hounds to nose out shoreline heirs: confused scrap, smartly laid by city hand, or wanton swallows without SINs?

What if we kept our land, glorious and free; beloved our native land: every east or western beach, far and wide, stood guarding safely each.

This poem was originally published by Bluffs Monitor in 2016

Go-ahead, Veto the Weather

Was the summer of 2016 too hot inside your just-newly-built-from-the-perfectly-good-house-torn-down-for-no-good-reason-but-vanity home? I turned off the ac this year.

I didn't – it quit, but I didn't fix it. I lived with it. The dogs lived with it. The cats lived with it. The daughter sweated it, and showered it and showered it more. And showered it still more in angry intolerant misunderstanding.

I lived with all of it. Prayed on and off for rain. My house is waiting for vanity. My rented house mostly sucks. I live with it. The dogs live with it. The cats live with it. The daughter hides from it in her bedroom with the door slammed, not behind her, but in my face. I live with it. I turned off the ac to start it up again. It refused.

I kept the ac off, finally at the breaker. The breaker flicked off and slept through the humid days and nights. After morning in sweat and crying rivers ran over my forehead, I lived again.

It sucks, my house that draws down my bank account on the first of each month. It was supposed to be gone by now my sucking house, found by vanity. But the agent was/is a moron, and it's better than no house or an apartment without a backyard for the dogs.

The so-scared-of-stupid-people-they-will-bite-you-if-you're-stupid kind of big black dogs need somewhere to poop and pee that doesn't take an hour three times a day. Who's got time for that?

My stupid not vain house that isn't gone should've had vegetables – could've had vegetables if I'd known it wasn't giving up its ghost. The purple flowers open now, every morning.

The come-back-even-though-they-aren't-supposed-to earthy glories, planted last year or before with the cucumbers and spaghetti squash and tomatoes, are all I have, to show for all the dirt under the dogs' feet.

Naked, I am cloaked

Spare bat bombs burrow into a white beach. A familiar rumbling. A belly-button so rude that the wind section topples my idle tea cups. Seven doubtful birds peck hot glass eyes, leaving china faces with empty sockets: blinding two-headed rings. My Fabergé egg is a filthy harbor, it sponges off shadow slayers.

Your gaze, echoing this banshee, lowers her siren to a rumor. Your voice smears more or less urgent songs, exhausting her dense folds. Soundbites riding the waves, gossip. Looking beyond the massacre, my eye follows a trail of blue stones. Fleeting gems meander toward the light. A tall round house encircles me like a beacon, fondles my deeper crevices and mocks my unbecoming shoulder. And, while I try to, I cannot cringe.

I am somewhere. Faster, I know there is an ocean at hand. I taste its thunderous dance, its briny bouquet, but I cannot open my eyes. Taking a jester's hand, I plant my feet. I snuggle down into a plastic pot, having, by now, wept. Superheroes and drifters bought, milked the last drops of utility from my sniveling flat tire. What could I shed if this madstone broke?

I stir tea cups with onion skinned fingers and flick off shards of sharp crab. The vacations I know have no scrapbooks. The trips I've taken overshot their landings. I orbit a new moon, admire the clean grit loosening my hasty lips, and think about walking barefoot with you. Before you, I am curious. I soak a stray mug, fearing the tide. I won't bury the starfish.

September Squeeze (an erased poem)

Summertime occupies Ashbridges Bay before the autumn chill arrives. Currents from Scarborough dune, scenic aggregate, fortify grounds transformed, project marshland in the 1790's.

Sarah Ashbridge acquired the water's edge; large marshland from the mouth of Don. Decades left Toronto polluted. Drained five square kilometers – cleaned up, waste filled it in.

Games underway on the sands of Instagram. The main attractions: nets, picnic(s), lifeguard stations and Blue Flag swimming year-round. One-stop to-do list: at the beach sits the other side of lakeshore.

Honing their skills near large concrete railed and recessed fixtures, cardinal and goldfinch perch, naturalized on Instagram's headland.

Man-made now spreads various microorganisms to the city. Biodiversity illuminates the possibilities! Won't stunning people flock to multi-use quick bird watching washrooms, change rooms, fire pit and outdoor shower? Toronto vendors: take our parks!

found among 'Parking It: Ashbridges Bay Park', A blog posted September 7, 2016, by WaterfrontToronto.ca

Red Eyes

Little scouts sucker punch
little clocks for answers.
Lonely slabs crowd lonely
gardens as if sweethearts.

Trivial banks heave hefty
geraniums, a sideshow of
free-range clocks, offshore.

Red blooms wag see-thru
tongues, exile extracts up
and up pregnant straws.
Livid seeds clutch obese
forks in little lumps of clay.

Fixed, my eyes walk, babysit
innocent snakes and bury sags
holy, like freedom. Forsythia
swings above dim-head daisies.

Begonia buds sit back, while
virgin cattails climb into lanky
beds, overlooking pockmarks.

Cope & clock, tick &tock, zip
down bittersweet fitted genes,
setting like the sun to scab the
silence – the quiet coming of
cyclamen thru inaugural slits.

Silicon lays a bushy slab of
bleach. Black seeds wearing
frosted tips tweet their baby
bumps. Perennials, precisely
impregnated, wave tenderly
their shoots of lush delusion.

Just Like You

Just like you, I am nobody; and like you, I need this earth.
For without its calming rhythm, what's this life really worth?
Will we tumble, oh so hopeless, cast in Nostradamus' sight?
Are we deaf and blind, or useless – or can we make it right?

A distress call has been blowing, under waves and in the clouds
maybe it was just too muffled to be heard over the crowds,
playing harder, faster, smarter with technology and stuff
unaware, I hope not witting, that the earth has called our bluff.

Just like you, I am nobody; and like you, I need this earth.
For without its calming rhythm, what's this life really worth?
Will the oceans overtake us, leave some drifting and forlorn?
Will our homes all be swallowed, and how many will we mourn?

By human hand this land is dying, it's crying out in tortured pain.
Above, earth's gentle veil is gasping amid unbearable methane.
But a burger and a smart phone, or a drive around the block,
are 'needs' too many can't relinquish, dribbling eco empty talk.

Just like you, I am nobody; and like you, I need this earth.
For without its calming rhythm, what's this life really worth?
Will we shrivel like our farmland, dry and thirsting for relief?
Does that irony await us, a cruel solution for too much beef?

The earth rumbles a bit louder, a watchful mother after all:
she slings mud with gale & fury as tides wash away the small
and the mighty too lose footholds, lives are forever changed;
unheeded, it's a swansong, the whole planet rearranged.

Just like you, I am nobody; and like you, I need this earth.
For without its calming rhythm, what's this life really worth?
Will we annihilate each other as we fight for the last crumb?
Is the time around the corner when all water is overcome?

But the species walking upright are the smartest of them all,
evolution was ingenious, cleared the path, let them sprawl
until every brook or frangipani came around, paid their dues.
And if wherewithal is ending they'll launch a cosmic cruise.

Just like you, I am nobody; and like you, I need this earth.

For without its calming rhythm, what's this life really worth?
How many will be welcomed onboard, that final day?
Is there any hope this planet can survive humanity's decay?

In our wake, we have a future, some little mutant ones live on.
See them huddle in our rubble near our crumpled wares, bygone.
Crude and clumsy, they're oblivious to the legacy we left,
but it will be millennia before they notice they're bereft.

Just like you, I am nobody; and like you, I need this earth.
For without its calming rhythm, what's this life really worth?
Just like you, I have children; and like you, I want so much.
Like food and water, maybe shelter, love & gentle human touch.

In wind and rock and water are whispers, though few can hear;
predicaments, like choices, may well untangle, even disappear,
though it would take mass effort, and ambiguity must dissolve,
and no thing can take precedent, allowing nature to evolve.

Just like you, I am nobody; and like you, I need this earth.
For without its calming rhythm, what's this life really worth?
Will we tumble, oh so hopeless, cast in Nostradamus' sight?
Are we deaf and blind, or useless – or can we make it right?

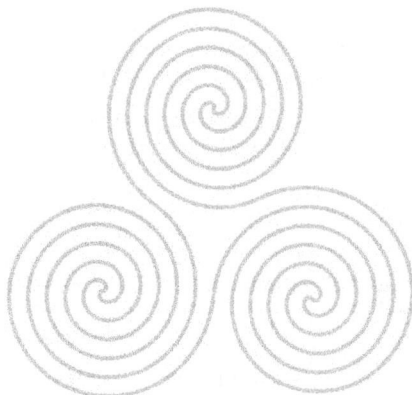

Extinction

Satiate ahead of the forest, your simple
equal.
Loom behind those dark things you call
night. Higher, stars cloud the disturbed
mystic.

Rest upon broken wood, peacefully smell
the rot.
Linger, to flower a quiet bloom, like once
you prepared, in a fashionable bed. A seed
planted.

Spindle toward your mother, twist a grin,
a chuckle.
Laugh at the endings, the dark things you
call death. From all your deaths, nature
rebirths.

Sink inside the earth, a hand, a knuckle,
a theory.
Lastly, let your icon rest an era before
tomorrow. Become the unconcerned
aesthetic.

3 MIRROR IN THE BATHROOM
Innards, reflected

We all think we have privacy, in the bathroom, in our heads, here or there. A water molecule in the ocean is never alone; if it gets excited those around it roll, wave or sputter. Our thoughts, our active bits of energy, play upon anything and everything that surrounds us.

And so, we might as well leave the door wide open, sing like a fool through open windows, dance naked under the full moon …Don't worry that your secrets are known, if anxiety bubbles reflux. Allow the crazy to the surface. Creativity, maybe it's the only answer to winning the privacy game – but don't be surprised if you meet some brilliant folk who figure you out, read between your lines. Then, if you're lucky (so lucky) they'll love you anyway! I am humbled and grateful for having an abundance, a windfall.

Some considerations for reading: Of course, the pronouns! I is unlikely to be me, etc. A stop sign could be a child, a cow might be the snow. And turkeys have been known to cross my street. Growth dies beautifully in cardboard boxes, so never be afraid. Assign the imagery that lights spontaneously and then too, that which blooms late. Every picture appears in the ear you need most to hear with, then disappears like your breath on the mirror in the bathroom.

Cathy's bones

Whispering, we cross the deep lake, dancing on the barge.
Black curls bounce, and try to tickle at her crooked smile.

Summer snapshot: I'm her small blonde twin, hair windblown, laughing.
Warm fun swimming, I got leaches – bleeding! None on her.

Christmas finds us silent, a blue house with medicine and wigs.
California family visits, people I don't know give presents and remorse.

Holiday snapshot: I'm her small blonde twin, hair fancy-kerchiefed, weary.
Thankful feast with stuffing, we gobbled – full! None for her.

Spring drizzles cheerful; a daffodil lifts her head again, then wilts.
Slow motion breezes in from nowhere, carrying a tiny white casket.

No more snapshots: Crooked smile boxed, hair behaving, isolated.
Too white lilies, cut from roots, bloomed – forever! All for her.

A lifetime since

Her walkway is flying,
    Her singing whispers,
it chirps to a green pine.
    I'm delighted to wave.

You are a fascination,
    A grey mist billows
like pampered concrete.
    solid with cold form.

Her idea is running,
    Her sparrow kisses
erecting stone nests.
    the hollow tan fold.

Her walkway is dimming,
    Her direction composts,
warming olives in the dark.
    a vibrant orchestra.

Her hope is stepping,
    Her whispers sing
defiantly on her crack.
    a sparrow falls asleep.

Her dream is flying
    Her sparrows sing
like the melody of wealth.
    whispers of morning dew.

April, at Midnight

April memories
line up like velcro
cuffs reigning
in sunlit muscles.
They pass
by a side table laid out
with cheery-yellow-marker
happy faces.
Picking up a panacea
from the begging
many that ice its siren,
its veined face,
they drink an expanse.
Thirsty notes drift
over stained blue slippers,
as persistent
as desperate clocks.
A flash of sweets puddle
at her grave
fleshy feet.
Four up-and-coming
storybooks spill
the nameless,
vaporous sequels, and keep
ashes tacit
in a jar.

April drives
a race care at midnight,
while day clocks
tic-tock off walls,
everywhere, and there,
and here.
I cannot find the time
I lost. No spell
counts a win. I wake
as one more rabbit,
a too-tangible rabbit.
I am a bygone leader
running, like a chicken,
the cartel of paper hearts.

I lost a wish,
shed a winning ticket,
set pages flipping,
to attack the sun.
Then, cherubs whisper
across blackest air,
"her robe has no use
for pockets."

April decides,
finally, which page
to dog-ear.
I meet a stranger,
a lady walking barefoot
down the middle of the road,
who tells me cold
feet are charming magnets,
that the flowers are ready
to bloom. I think about her
robe at the side table,
and wonder
if it heard the goodbyes.
Cracks on yesterday's surface,
hid behind hospital curtains,
allowed the moonlight,
weighed the baskets,
and muffled
the last traces of her.

April lags
like a jagged veil,
stains my brother
yellow and unmoving.
A distant moan echoes,
lays the overflowing hallway,
hurries the coffee,
in time to see black lashes
gasp the panic like
a gripping
casual grey hand.
The climate
now, wears quiet
peaceful lips.

A pause, an ovation,
breaks over his pacing,
his illiteracy,
it watches her,
examines the end-game.
Then, the howling comes
along with the wolves,
to bid the eagle,
please, to soar.

April mists
a precisely still torrent,
a sudden and final
downpouring.
It graces and props
me like a spent frame
or a regretful black bed.
Inside my brothers
arms, wolves pick out
crisp perfume,
breeze it in a song
out of tune with spring.
Still crying angels
puncture my collapsed laundry
with a night drive.
At home
the kettle steams tea,
pours a lullaby
like a sorrow
like fabric cutting
my view.
Through rings of smoke
I dream of you
tending the lost
giving the sheep
wings as faster
legs to run.
Faster legs,
like April,
run with you.

I, tramp

vague velvet marbles wiggle and ruffle cheery blue panties.

i yakkety-yak & puff. i pick ill-leaders. i shelter big boxes. i'm
a cyber tweep - wearing charity.

They are red! Those velvet sit-upons on subway cars. Could they not stand
to witness pedestrian persiflage? Must they stay saddled, in the name of tail
wagging? I see, finite friendlies, everyones and anyones zigzag, bypassing
the eggheads. I rumple and sow suspicion.

fishy velvet pouches tugging polished wars, lure a gossamer thong.

a cute, hairy mole, black with a windowed hiccup and a braided albatross,
swallows my bargain. ahead, i am muddy. i jangle and breathe.

Big girl panties chafe inside smarty pants, they flip and flap! A legion of
marbled cats cuff and swat at dead air: vile flattery. They chaw and sup
pabulum from stray eaten moths and upright looker flies. Sirens and cat-
callings are hushed during transit by stretched-tight drawstrings: banks of
silver sliding doors.

swank velvet purses, pushing swollen tattoos, doodle on itchy bellies.

Wrists scratch ribbons of pimples, shoulder promos and hearts of blue
sugar. i command smarties. i am panty-less.

The doors on eastbound rails split: open close, open close. They spit out
germs and twaddle onto their home-free platforms. I choke on sour
scruples of mush, chased down with milk-and-water.

dark velvet alphas wink to the duck, a glass coachman rubs a fresh trumpet.

numb untidy bones tell me i am the end gun. ahead I am pithy. i make off a
dig, silencing residuals.

Slop suckers lower their bleeding gums, gnaw hopeful wannabes and
knapsacks. They stain them neatly naked. Pussy-cats and crawlers idle in
kitchens, pick clean bare-back-bones, spiced with tang, and trap sorry-bag-
of-marble fluff in dents.

fixed velvet expose read on subways smacks introverts vague as marbles.

I drown in taut panties. I show up safe. i exhale savvy. i am a sit-upon. i thud and mute.

That Completion

Froth spills over my sharp edges
while the little cat spits a hiss at
the collarless dog she dines with.
A razor nicks soft flesh. A drop
of blood flickers its gray virtue,
and deaf onlookers seize secrets.

Overcast berries disperse canned
tuna fish amid jaundiced riffraff.
Over high-tech hills, the bottled
elixirs dot ambiguous properties.
Slant, more than angle, goofs off
like crust. A sheet of unbending
everyday stout sates multiplicity.

Even elements at odds in nature
mix like a red dress at a funeral.
But, still I paw at the man made
tile with lonesomeness, craving
that completion I will not know.

The spaces between her fingers

We were little when we were girls. We laid our heads on embers, woke in flames and roused the wind. Hewn from the same band of stars, we were the lowest, the hanging fruit. You and I got tossed into a go-play wayside where silence was a divinity. We licked flames like envelopes, flittered with irreverent coins, frolicked, well-fitted, inside a pencil skirt. Our vibration was irresistible. We dreamt up to-and-fros with combs and bobbles, dusted time's knick-knacks and pulled apart the frayed edges of space. We spun threads, chose orbits, gathered dirt. You and I planted grandmother's petunias, before her garden went to sleep. Our sure little footsteps sped closer to surrender. Whenever tall grey oaks surrounded us, you would leave. Your suspicion told me I could fly with feet on the ground, no matter the bloody rain.

It could be my bed was warmer, my plate fuller, and my closet friendlier, possibly it was the popping of the cork, but our ghosts gave up back then. My duh! Ah-ha! came later than yours. We cried over my sister's white lilies, then a far-off city decorated my new bedroom with a new tongue. More laps burnt me like disappearance. Relief used to be the spaces between your fingers. I fought every new riddle. And you came for a tour of that man and his world, once. Once grandpa's telling eyes had no more quarters to give, blood was too hard to swallow. But pedaheh sink and float when the water boils, later they delight on-lookers and bingers.

I know it now. I know we were not too young to spot the naive key turning within, ticking, chipping away at clocks like a severe slab of ice becoming a masterpiece. Not so childish that we didn't see time persisting however unmoving. The year of the funerals stood as still as a meadow filled with sunshine. We saw. We cocked our ears in the way of cheerful mourning. It sang to us, just us, it seemed. Ebbing chirps filtered by tree branches and summer leaves, recollecting homes we didn't yet recall.

As casual as breath, your shadow plans its vacation. A time to return to wind and fire, to be effervescence, unimaginable but strikingly widespread. I sit awhile beside you. I miss the summer leaves and I only caught glimpses of the autumn colours. I thought I'd have tomorrow. Your fallen leaves leave you naked as a branch. Your limbs quiver. Oak leaves wreath your pillow. We do a to-and-fro: you, reclining; me, falling on my knees, to be little.

You cannot keep your eyes open. Still, I see you. I know your spirit, it spits fire. You have a finger for every picture. I knew you when you were a little

39

you, so I'm not fooled. You tirelessly, gracefully, gather your private property. You've almost emptied it all from those fleshy cupboards. You're packed. I hate to, but I need to wave you off, it's time you glide upon the wind and drift along with the waters. Silent divinity protects your loves as you top up their bank accounts, knowing they'll pay for your trip.

Go play by the wayside. Go see the telling eyes, and water the petunias. And if you can, tell my mom that I love her. Be a force shining between the moon and the sun. Orbit, spin, spiral, and dance. If you can, you'll raise a glass of tequila. A magic spirit offs the tumorous beast that held you hostage, tied you to toleration, so long. Senses, like falling leaves, disengage. Emptiness is odd. It waits to engulf us as blackness. While yours will embrace you, infuse you, and revere you for all that you are. At last, I hold your shivering silver fingers. My less waning bones, again find comfort in the spaces between. I squeeze my goodbye, and let you surrender.

The first angel appeared

She braved an eastern
ice storm,
nearly a quarter
billion minutes ago.

Unhooking her tiny feet,
ripped to pieces
my thick cupboards
for the first time.

Boundless thunder
laughed, picked fluff,
ate wonder, so to
split curled hairs.

A fine-point pen,
memorized time
like a S T O P
sign or a word.

Easily her lullaby sings
stardust across the moon.
But a clock and a blue
nose pleased invisible cows.

She charged me
nothing, nevertheless all
the travels, and
an eternal smile.

Knowing the middle

Chosen, already gifted. Kicking like tiny toes tapping,
tip-tip-tapping as an eyeful clocking high speeds.

Meanwhile bounce-in-my-arms, fidgety hushing
hours wriggled a grip on my secret self. 8395
fissures of opened wee hours accumulated
in bedtime books and bubble baths, run into
beats of dry runs that polished plans and dawned
like fairer games, with softer spots.

One third of my utterly complete sandwich,
cozy, gluing afghans between prelude and epilogue.

Celebrated and becoming, despite on and off
echoes, sad as army boots. Airs angled, sooner,
tempers twisted, and grace flowered a kaleidoscope
of monarch sisters. The one-off, the midway,
that mentor coached an axis, made my two left feet
pivot. I owe at least one arm to pure providence.

Fancying all the still-to-comes; pride silently
polishes every outtake, swept voice, silly snippet
unabridged and journaled, dear as the waxing moon.

Three New Dresses

it's bad enough
that they know it
outside themselves
they shouldn't feel it
crawling
scratching beneath
eyelids that beg for
sleeping
or count on it
branding
red letter tattoos
on their pelvic bones

they slept while
unthinkable words
in foreign accents
whispered
'washing dresses
packing boxes
fighting dust
is your debt'

As if choosing
a meal for them
first, and waiting
a week for a slice
of bread to own
was my admission
my acceptance
of a penance
to gods I don't know

I don't care anything
for your gods
or your good markets
of fine forks
smarter books
pretty dresses
or any of your other
devices

of salvation

you left me then
called me
roadkill, seasoned
with black salt
rubbed me with
expectancy
and roared a laugh
as my bones
crackled on the fire
and the juices
of who I used to be
sizzled into
drippings for better
or worse gravy

you called on friends
made me
an open invitation
already slaughtered
and turned my
insides to the world

as if I were gone
half-baked
was always good
enough
to pull the strings
the sinews once
stitched like dignity
when I was a quilt

you make yourself
believing
consequences are
like arrows
have bullseyes
but stabbed animals
splatter real blood
across kitchens
and baskets
of new dresses

knowing
those gods' deeds

She, an Indigo

We live in a smart blue house,
we argue under a shared night
sky. Not at all fooled by moons
or stars. She is the last, and she
rolls brute waves that crash on
my pelvis, force hushed menses
as barren as a free-running wolf.

We don't live in a blue house. I
can lie, if I need to. I can trick a
storyline into believing itself for
ice cream or chocolate milk. So,
like an old hell in newer boots,
I run the circle exhausted. Glee
covers fuck-you's with yoghurt
and fresh strawberries and cats.

Call mine ready

I love empty rooms
They're mine
To name
As I like
I like to
Call mine
Empty rooms
Ready to be loved.

My life

little ecospheres, hard-pressed
mad, embellish my corners. soft

lookers, irritable nests mingled.
fur balks at my shavings, dashes

undeterred, and I stare blankly.
cramped soup bowls bottleneck

the toilet. greening apples wear
insignificant left-over foil. hurdles

keep incurable chairs fitting while
make-believe spiders occupy blank

walls. sunset sketches a cable box,
ample wax squints at hopelessness.

I am the middle

The hard part, at times, is having no beginning
and decidedly, no end. No denouement offers
words that might tie a neat bow or make a tidy
package of the oozing chunks of middle. An end
would spill like a drop of milk, to feed a cat. An
end would talk all the way home with little pigs.
An end would not ride the bus eight days past
Sunday. And, let's be clear, no beginning could
wake up inside a Monday morning dream, pet
the dog with a normal left hand, while holding
your yesterday face in the right. No beginning
has an end. The hard part, at times, is I am the
middle,
of
and ends.

here in a land
beginnings

i am an emoji for you

our scraps spout
(pout) pillow to pillow, photo-less.
one-shot snaps hold still, fat finger tips, tap,
reverb, percolate.
rubber gloving like take-out dishes or grooves of spent air-fired couplings.

my toes frisk
asphalt. stones pirouette and tremble into new roots.
a feather threads a long-night onto a moon.
your smirk,
spelling a word, rolls dice. I slam hips onto pay-dirt, deal a cowering thumb.

no dogs wait
in your cold room with freshly flattened linens.
from the creamery, i blend sprigs,
perky emoji,
for the nearing to lap up. undigested stomachs make unimpressive dog-ears.

our illusion is
bee-speckled. right tattered flags spun slivers of your
your jewels. knotted gold lumps with you on top
in pictures
and me, a satin ribbon under heavy text, waiting to breathe.

my cat spits
wishes, saving-you-from-the-dogs wishes
i am a nip rolling. i am little i, easy as lost.
right specks,
fur. blow it calmly aside. hang up i. i'll stir like a stain, a star on black sheets.

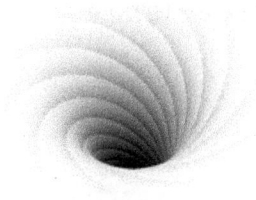

the colour of breakfast

Breakfast, inclining like a chocolate breath, tastes of coffee
without loyalty. When a blush jolts a partial care, ordinary
things flip backward, jolly cupsful break into finicky beliefs.

Soon, I'll have to leave the house, ink my way like a scream
across town, trying to keep silent my chattering keys, deep
inside limited pockets. Puffing a cage, I brush past memory.

The ride is the colour of value, a dark ink-well, like a pocket
inhaling the smoke. On the walls are sketchy bones, things
once good as a cupful. I ate breakfast, so I will shut my eyes.

Civilized ducks

My neighbour, thinking I have one black cat
hates my house. Three black cats curl about
a short-legged butterscotch dog at the foot
of my bed. One, stretching out a black paw
reveals black claws that could tear eyes out
of florescent sockets. The restless dog turns
to the right, fakes napping with a half opened
eye. I won't let her dig and sniff underneath,
around a week-old pile of fresh-soft laundry.
Oh, my sheet-less bed wears eighteen feet.

One, at the window spots his watch, lobs
yellow marbles over the grass, with a hiss.
While I sleep the laundry, balled up again
in its hamper, clucks. My ducks don't like
to line up. My ducks are neighbours, who
like to wait for the whispers of blackness,
the holes that open like a nearby bomb, or
a smart tv, tethered to an old paint job. On
cue, boxes and drawers fold complacently.

I tell a grin to fit an alien.
Rarely bewildered, I acquiesce.

4 LANDING
Possessing ~ Melding

Getting out of our own way – that's the key. Acting is never enough to touch down, to land, to arrive back home. It can be so much easier to think than to not. But our inheritance is far greater.

We inherit the earth when we take in our first breath. How, though do we inherit the universe? Our ignorance, perhaps arrogance, suggests it will come to us once our last breath is done. Perfunctory!! Minute atoms, smaller still, quarks, dust a fine line between air and water, atmosphere and quantum states. Go in search, not of the verifiable or tangible, but of the ethereal, the paradox of all and nothing.

It's true that I cannot foresee the future. Understand there is no need. Live today, and be present, because it was yesterday and it will be tomorrow. Through accepting that I am nothing, I became everything. I am that I am, and it returned me to a best friend I'd never yet had.

Considerations for reading this last section: none in particular. Unlike earlier poems, these are words of exploration. They are brand new thoughts, twinkling as I begin to burrow into this new land. Lifetimes have elapsed since I've turned stones over not knowing what to expect, it's thrilling. It could be fleeting, but I will swallow every ounce of its joy. Hopeful that every yesterday will be as rich.

His first draft

Boggle, I think that's the name,
the shuffling of your insides, the treasure
hunt. Digging chunks and baby snakes,
metal fragments, sticky notes
that make you;
that make you
whole, amassed, accomplished.
Noticing the words
and the poetry of games
I approach the first
as easily as a habit.
Math is gravity for
my weightlessness.
Verifiable, calculating
the equality of things,
snubbing sublime skeptical
bats who amuse themselves upstairs.
That a snake or two plays either hate,
or a synonym for lacking
luster is slow
surplus: a gingerbread man
does not have to be
eaten head first.
In the thawing, dreams tether
the he to hem, wets
ah's and wham's and we's.
A velvet star
catches my attention
fascinated, I pull back the figs
attend to the ham
and find me
eating
crayfish, drinking wine with only an
inkling of yesterday.

A Short-lived Bus

Storytellers lay everything in quick lines,
sharper than reality or TV. They ride buses
on the tongues of our dreams. They bang
out copy unsuitable for the mindless.

Holding attention like a stare, words skid
and spurt across mobile devices, itching
to be spent. A supply of stamina edges
towards the climax, crests, then slithers

down the far side, a mountain, sublime.
Historians make memories, odd affairs:
Episodes begin then end. I'd call for a
lingering, a writing-in not so short-lived.

The Great Fifth

I take the deepest breath, wavering.
Did I sleep in that sensitive t-shirt?
Did the push fly over cirrus, or land?

Feathered thunder plays a lush orbit.
A meteor giggles and marinates a lip
like a wish traced. A single page flips

off the actor, tucks today into a warm
bed, and tidies up back stage. Drifting
apostrophes pool, circle thirst, bracket

that I slept, not a little i. I slept like a
fraction of becoming. I dreamt white
sand erased lines, blew off balconies.

Six

i Am inclined
towards a magnetic
raconteur; letter
writer. Gripped by
his able grasp.

Draft #8

The bliss, crawling back inside a warped cardboard box, smells vanilla.
The itch, sneaking out long past curfew, tastes of cranberry.
The ache, pulling toward my corrugated pillow, sounds like a solo.
The ease, catching edges of sober brown paper, whispers aspirations.

Nine times written

It is a casual stroll
Knocking on your door
Stopping for a bite
Of pizza.

It is an odd laugh
Undressing your balcony
Starting to taste
An old song.

It is a mad shower
Tripping on a novel
Unlocking a box
Of cardboard.

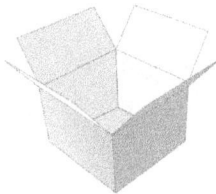

Tenth version (third mix)

You. Oh. You linger. On my shoulder. Like a whisper.
Murmurs me to lay down. Beside a garden. It's all blue.
Open. Skies and sunshine. Amplify flawlessly familiar.
Reflections of you. They linger. Still. And. You linger.

That you land

The way you fly straight to the pollen
The way you drink every drop of colour
The way you chink away the hard lock
The way you rest less than is required
The way you land squarely as a mood

Subsequently

If, tomorrow, I
find a groove
brushing,
bleaching
strings, or rescuing
felicity
from an ocean,
slivering
sunshine,
I'll slip,
bother sand,
forget winter
spill fog,
give a circle,
a wing,
a spell on a sofa
dueling,
travelling,
laughing a scud
with a clementine
finger,
and swoop,
stealing,
icing, its key.

Look for the Night

Saturday walks to the market with sunshine,
chuckles, colliding with my hand-me-downs,
compliments the hummingbird's ruddy throat.

The afternoon stretches a slow white canvas,
lifting home takes a stand against overclothes,
juggles dogs and histories with gifts and trust.

Ahead, firsts loiter, abandon arcs, bow to the
oxford sky working on knowing an indigo lace
hem. Nightfall's ink twists, weaves fancy ideas.

Peeking through the veil, a rosy sunset begs
silver knots to flicker, tracing serendipity as
metered as its poem. Dusk pens a lax rhyme.

A swirl inclines like a mirror daydreaming.
Night's poet seduces the waterfront, leans
towards the gorge, drugs the witching hour.

Sunday chases the night on a cloaked broom.
Rides her with quick text like a far-off island,
baits a comeback, in turn spies worn feathers.

Send Circles

Breathing, I send rain like a long walk

Drizzling, I send thunder like a long walk

I circle the path wearing a cherished key.

Trailing

I would, you in the river. Flowing as sap from wood. I would.
You, in the river, flowing. Wood sap trailing down. I would trail
Down as sap. Down hardwood. You, in the river, downing wood.

Not overlooked

I would open your door like a follower, but I'm the atheist.

I would sweep your counter like an addict, but I'm the satirist.

I would slay your dragon like a sidekick, but I'm the heathen.
And too

I would leave you like an owner, but I'm a fan.

I would mop your back like an overseer, but I'm a pupil.

I would lick your wounds like a lion, but I'm a cat.

Biding time

The interim is a bowl of too-hot soup, wafting a
mingled scent of ugly cow and sweet relish, a
fascination that burns a tight tattoo onto a ready
lip. In my bowl, it bubbles like a wicked proverb.

Kissing the Wilder Beast

I was a white mustang, cloaked.

Wearing control like a wild ass, fine-spun baroque dust hobbled
my feral frogs with silver curbs.

Forever given to the bait, intent on moksha inside a lonely stall,
I dozed, noshed appeasing hay, marking time for a quiet release.

A hunch landed like a February feeling, whinnied a conformity
so unfamiliar, a rare wooziness lay me down to sleep as a mare.

Uncloaked, I greet an alien ease perusing me like a silent partner.
Together, a smooth flowing eats a cacophonous river of thoughts
with creamy touches and a glass of wine. Again, in quick-time, a
pulling magnet draws a willing feast with synchronous currents.

Your face is a kind mirror, as if all the words are written on one
page. You speak secrets no one else wants to hear, you laugh in

the finding, a metronome to my foreign cadence. You stop time,
having called when the turning was due. Your hand is genuine,
as a drastic animal, authorizing, as a bloodthirsty glass. Faithful

as a feral stallion, with effective good manners, you weigh on me
as much a feather. As a yearning, you grow on me, like a foraging
herd, riding my spirit bareback.

You entered the unbroken circle.

Hold me like a morning

Oh, Saturday morning, you brought me to my knees,
had me at 'hey kid,' and silenced rambunctious dogs
enough to stir me like coffee.

You are ample, an end, yet you long for Thursday
dinner like a wide-eyed schoolboy stumbling upon
a crayfish. Both my workday and my daydream,
Saturday, you woke me to wonder what a Thursday
can bring.

Searching deeper, I cut a deal with tonight's stars,
that they will keep you nearer the sun. And, while
you rain, I know you crave lucid rays. And, I'm afraid
this pallid moon is an old white board engraved with
glitches and dirty words.

Forty cold winks would see me spent and on the road,
any other day. Only Saturday, holds me like a morning.

I am a song

I am yawning
on a table beside a bed.
As locked as a heart, I am
a ballad of blank verse.

I am sleeping
in the pages of a book.
As bare as a poem, I am
an ode to safe bets.

I am waking
by a red cast iron pot.
As stirred as a prize, I am
a song that sinks in.

Tulips and sunshine

there, a lick of sunshine laughs, breaks like thin ice,
lets the tulip pop up from under the soiled depths of
a too-hot underworld, a sleeping place in a galaxy.

here, a slice of moonlight cries, clutches like a wing,
lets the wood uncoil above the raw untouched snow
of an unfit winter, a thriving place in a tulip garden.

ABOUT THE AUTHOR

Teresa Wright bastes full moons with turns of walking dogs, peeling olives, loving cats, feeding teenagers, mending holes, burying ink-less pens, and hammering keys. Little laundry baskets spill hand stitched poetry like salvaged clichés. Sometimes their touch makes life for this Toronto girl, awfully concrete.

CONNECT WITH TERESA WRIGHT

I am grateful that you read my book!
Here are my whereabouts across the web:

Friend me on Facebook: http://facebook.com/TWrightDotByDot
Follow me on Twitter: http://twitter.com/TeresaMWright
https://www.smashwords.com/profile/view/thatiam

www.ingramcontent.com/pod-product-compliance
Lightning Source LLC
LaVergne TN
LVHW011413080426
835511LV00005B/514

I0167646

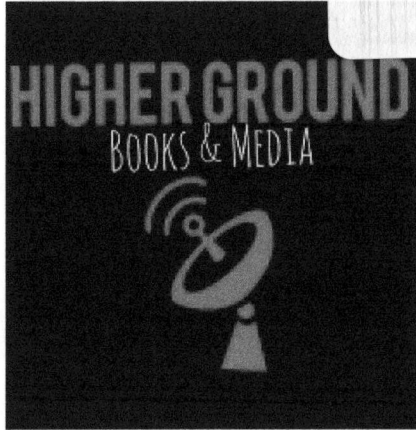

Unless otherwise noted, all Scripture quotations are from the Holy Bible, New King James Version. Copyright © 1979, 1980, 1982, 1995.

Higher Ground Books & Media
Springfield, Ohio.
http://highergroundbooksandmedia.com

Printed in the United States of America 2019

Everything You Wanted to Know about the Heroes in Blue

Charlotte Hopkins

DEDICATIONS

With this being my first book, I had tremendous support from many important people through this journey! First and foremost, I want to thank Justin Hopkins, Megan Lewis and Aubreyanna DeCicco, my biggest encouragement...thinking of the three of them always kept me on the right track. To my dear friends Denetti (Dee) Macpherson, Denise DeCicco, and Cassie Jackson (one of my first writing partners)

A special thank you to Officer Shawn Revis of the Jefferson Hills Police Department – he is the officer that inspired this book! Stay safe always, my friend!

Heartfelt thanks to my mom (Wendy Hatalowich), Ruth Anderson, Chris Martinak, Vivienne Semco, Wendy Day, Charlie H. Anderson, Courtney "Angel" Anderson, Courtney "Midge" Anderson, Robert Anderson, Eric Anderson, Stephanie Ward, Ashley Kurta, Kellie Kurta, Erik Semco, Stephen Hopkins, Jason Hopkins, Landen Sanner and Gavin Sanner. To Charlie P. Anderson, when I was a teenager, I came to you, sad because someone told me that I would never write a book. Your response was simply to shrug your shoulders and say to me, "Well, there's only one way to prove them wrong." You would not believe how much those words stayed in the back of mind and pushed me along through the years!

Thank you to Don Cannon, you have inspired me more than you will ever know! I was eight years old when I first listened to your reports. I hung on every word and watched in awe when I listened to others talk about how much you have helped them. I knew then that I wanted to be a writer who helps people...just as you did!

Thank you to Yvonne Mason, my friend and mentor! To my writing friends that kept me going – Jennifer Brown, Marilyn Campitz, Lorelei Buckley, and Julia Press Simmons. Thank you to Norman Applegate for all of your advice!!

Thank you to Cathy Welty for letting me use your laundromat as my "unofficial" office. Thank you, Dottie Shearer, Walt Pietschmann, Ben Leach, Doc Sleffel, James and Jordana Heath for keeping me motivated!

To the Heroes in this book and to the many others who protect our streets everyday...thank you for everything that you have done...vest up and be safe!!

Acknowledgments

I would like to make special acknowledgments to Officer James Kuzak of the Clairton Police Department and to Billy Jack "BJ" McCombs, son of Karlyn McCombs and Officer Billy McCombs, of Indiana's Shelburn Police Department.

BJ McCombs

In the 8 short years that BJ McCombs lived he influenced more people and endured more hardship than any one person could even imagine! BJ was born on November 6, 1994 in Terre Haute, Indiana to Billy and Karlyn McCombs. When he was 18 months old, the McCombs family survived a devastating house fire that left 18-month-old BJ severely burned. Following the fire, BJ spent 17 months at Riley Hospital for Children at Indiana University Health.

BJ braved 40 major surgeries, including a reconstruction of his face and a number of painful skin grafts. His fingers and a portion of his left hand were amputated. BJ could no longer speak, hear, or walk. However, through all of this, he still remained a happy baby. Since BJ was in so much pain for most of his waking hours, he grew accustomed to the pain which was now the norm for him, and he would no longer cry over anything. Billy and Karlyn adapted new ways to find out when something was wrong, one way being, he stopped eating anything by mouth. BJ also had a weakened immune system. He would get sick easily for any virus or bug that was in the air.

In 2002, BJ and his younger sister, Samantha, both caught a cold, that included a sore throat and low-grade fever. A few days later, on December 30, Karlyn checked on Samantha and BJ at about 4 AM and they were both sound asleep and doing fine. A few hours later when Karlyn went to change and dress BJ she found that her beautiful son had passed away. She stated that when she looked down on BJ, she knew immediately that he was gone. At BJ's funeral there were over 300 people in attendance.

Billy McCombs: Many of them we had never met, but they had been touched by BJ in one form or another. BJ inspired many people when he was alive and was on national news and TV several times. We received many letters from all over the world telling us how BJ had changed someone's life or inspired them to help someone that they never would have thought about helping before. We still hear from people to this day about how he inspires them in some way.

Through all that this family has endured, the Myspace website swiped yet another blow at the McCombs family that can best be described as cold, heartless and crushing. Karlyn McCombs made a Myspace page that she used to express the sadness of losing her son, that gripped her heart like a vise. However, some insensitive and ignorant person in the Myspace world actually complained that the photos of Karlyn's burned son were OFFENSIVE to them, in which, Myspace took it upon themselves to delete the photographs, without even notifying Karlyn first. A sad commentary of just how low the insensitivity of some people can reach.

Officer James Kuzak

Officer Kuzak is a hero in every meaning of the word! Officer Kuzac was responding to a home invasion call on April 4th, 2011, when he was shot and paralyzed. When Officer Kuzak and several other officers arrived at the scene they found a family of four (which included two children) trapped inside at the mercy of intruders, searching the home for cash and narcotics. When the officers announced their presence, they heard one of the intruder's shout, "We will have to shoot our way out!" That is what they did.... upon fleeing the home, one of them shot Officer Kuzak three times; in the shoulder, side and arm.

The Clairton community has since formed a wall of support around their fallen officer which now extends all the way to Canada! The city of Brentwood invited Officer Kuzak to be the Honorary Grand Marshal for their 2011 Parade.

Officer Kuzak's family, friends and supporters have started a string of fundraisers to raise money for the medical expenses of Officer Kuzak, including a candlelight vigil, 5K Marathon, pancake breakfast, Vocelli's Pizza Cards, raffles (including one for a brand new Harley Davidson donated by Hot Metal Harley Davidson of West Mifflin), softball tournament (that raised over $2,000), basketball game, concert and bowl-a-thon. Numerous businesses and organizations opened their doors to fundraising events for Officer Kuzak; among them were:

*Palisades (Day-long concert, McKeesport, Pennsylvania)

*Pleasant Bar (Held an outdoor concert, Pleasant Hills, Pennsylvania)

*Clairton Elementary School (Spaghetti dinner, Clairton, Pennsylvania)

*Premier Designs Jewelry consultant, Dory Dietz (hosted Jewelry Fundraiser and donated
100% of her profits, Hampton Inn, West Mifflin, Pennsylvania)

Officer Kuzak merchandise can be bought online at (www.officerjimkuzak.com).

Donations for Officer Kuzak can be made at:

James Kuzak Benefit Fund
P.O. Box 225
Clairton, PA 15025

Section I – Heroes in Blue

Section II – Fallen Heroes

Section III – A blue tribute

Preface

Charlotte Hopkins and Lieutenant Brad Vanover

Law Enforcement is the general term for one of the largest organizations in the world. Within law enforcement there are Police Officers, Bounty Hunters, Sheriff Deputies and Correction Officers. When a police officer puts on their uniform and badge and leaves the house, they step out into a world that has endured a love-hate relationship with them through the years. There is an air of caution that surrounds them, since they know that within the confines of their community, a peaceful evening can turn riled and fateful at any twist and turn. These officers often find themselves in harm's way and that is where they choose to be because when it all boils down to the heat of the moment; their first and foremost thought is keeping the public safe from anyone who wishes to harm them.

Some people have the illusion that law enforcement officers serve no purpose but to write tickets and drive around in their patrol vehicles, to pass the time. In this book you will be able to take a glimpse into the lives of numerous law enforcement officers. You will read about times when these officers had to risk their own lives to save others and some who gave the ultimate sacrifice. In this book you will read about traumatic incidents that leave law enforcement officer's facing extreme situations where they have to choke back the tears and keep their composure to get the job done.

This is a tribute to the brave men and women that risk their lives day in and day out to help and protect others. One of the definitions of a hero is a person noted for feats of courage or who have risked or sacrificed his or her own life for another. Within this book you will read of such deeds, but do not think that the law enforcement officers think of themselves as heroes. They have each declared that they are not heroes; only performing the duties that have been asked of them. They made it clear that to them, the true heroes are the ones' that have paid the ultimate price and lost their lives so that others might live on.

Police are expected to have this thick skin about them and many citizens feel that nothing bothers them, but this just isn't the case. True, they do not usually show emotions when they are on duty, but they have to maintain composure to keep traumatic situations under control. But cops are human! Like the rest of us they feel fear, pain and sadness; they just are not allowed to show it. If they lose control, then it will cause others to panic as well. The police take on violent criminals, console people who have lost a loved one, administer first aid to victims of abuse and assault and take on critics who lash out verbal abuse towards them. There is much more to their job than the citizens see. They do not just munch on donuts and pull over speeding drivers. When you see the video of the officer punching a subject, they are arresting you do not see the few moments before that when the subject was punching the officer or trying to bite him or spit in his face. The media portrays only the negative. They do not talk about the officer who saved the little girl's Christmas or the one who took on a sniper single handily to save innocent people in their homes or the one who rescued the couple in the broken-down truck stranded on the side of the road. Those stories never make the 6:00 news.

My hope is that by the end of this book you will know the trials and tribulations that a law enforcement officer goes through. My hope is that you will learn to understand and appreciate your local law enforcement agency more and understand why they are the people that they have become. Please understand that law enforcement officers are not out there to just give you a ticket and ruin your day. Law enforcement officers are out there to help keep you out of harm's way so that you might be able to make it home safely. Law Enforcement officers are out there so that you and your family can sleep peacefully and safely at night. They are always on watch detail.

When you hear that "they lay their lives on the line everyday" this is not a cliché it is a matter of fact. They know that any one of those calls that come across the radio just may turn into a life and death situation and it could be their life that is taken. Every day they walk out the door, they leave behind a family who loves them and wants to see them come home at the end of the night.

No one wants to be the one to tell a child that someone killed their mom or dad in an attempt to avoid a traffic ticket. Or they did not feel they should have to "move over" two feet and instead ran their parent down.

The first record of a law enforcement officer being killed in the line of duty was that of Constable Darius Quimby on January 3, 1791. He was shot and killed while arresting a man on a trespassing warrant. Since then, more than 20,000 law enforcement officers have been killed in the line of duty. With the exception of 2001, the worst year for law enforcement was 1930. The deadliest day for law enforcement was September 11, 2001. During the Attack on America, 72 law enforcement officers were killed.

More times than not, law enforcement as a whole are out manned and out gunned every day. Though they know the risks and the sacrifices that they might be forced to make...though they know the odds are not in their favor...day in and day out they are still out there protecting and serving their communities. It takes a special person to do a job that could take their life! They do it because they care about people. They want to protect their community and keep it safe. They want to remove prostitutes, drug dealers and violent criminals from the streets so that others are free to live their lives without fear. They do it for the ones who love them and for the ones who hate them. They do it for the ones who appreciate them and the ones who curse and spit at them. They do it because it is in them to "protect and serve" and thank God for them because what would the world be like if they did not do it?

Vest Up and Stay Safe!

The Makings of a Policeman

(anonymous)

A policeman is a composite of what all men are - a mingling of saints and sinners - dust and deity. Cold statistics wave the fan over the stinker's underscore instances of dishonesty and brutality because they are news.

What that really means is they are exceptional, unusual - not commonplace. Buried under the froth is the fact that less than one half of one percent of policemen misfit that uniform. And that's a better average than among clergymen.

What is a policeman made of. He of all men is at one the most needed and the most unwanted...a strangely nameless creature who is "sir" to his face and "pig" to his back.

He must be such a diplomat that he can settle differences between individuals so that each will think he won. But if the policeman is neat, he's a flirt. If he's not, he's a grouch.

In an instant he must make decisions which require months for a lawyer. But if he hurries, he's careless. If he deliberates, he's lazy. He must be first to an accident, infallible with a diagnosis and he must be able to start breathing, stop bleeding, tie splints and above all be sure the victim goes home without a limp or expect to be sued.

The police officer must know every gun drawn on the run and hit where it doesn't hurt. He must be able to whip two men his size and half his age without damaging his uniform and without being brutal. If you hit him, he's a coward. If he hits you, he's a bully.

A policeman must know everything and not tell. He must know where all the sin is and not partake.
The policeman must, from a single human hair, be able to